Tax Cuts and Jobs Act
Your guide to the 2018 tax law

"What's in it (and out of it) for me?"

Julie L. Gentile, CPA, MBT, MBA

Patrick H. McCloskey, CPA, JD

DEDICATION

We dedicate this book to the American taxpayer. Although we may not always agree with how our tax dollars are spent, we still live in the land of opportunity, and we must always remember that only we have the power to make a change.

Table of Contents

ACKNOWLEDGMENTS

Call us crazy, but we love helping our clients tackle new and challenging projects and problems. We thank them for their loyalty, their referrals and their friendship. We are blessed to have such a great family of clients, and we hope to spend many more years providing them with the exceptional service they deserve.

DISCLOSURE

IRS Circular 230 notice: In order to comply with requirements imposed by the IRS, we must inform you that any U.S. federal tax advice contained in this publication is not intended or written to be used, and cannot be used, for the purpose of (i) avoiding penalties under the Internal Revenue Code or (ii) promoting, marketing or recommending to another party any transaction or matter that is contained in this publication.

This publication will also fail to make you rich, help you lose weight, whiten your teeth or regrow hair that has been lost. We cannot guarantee dates or life matches (in fact, if your friends find out that you read tax books, it could have a negative impact.) We have never given any good stock tips (that we have been told), we cannot buy your gold, and we do not have any insight into that Nigerian inheritance, left to you by the Prince.

CHAPTER 1

TAX REFORM

President Abraham Lincoln pushed the first income tax through congress in 1862 to help fund the Union Army. The tax rate was 3% on income over $500 and 5% on income over $10,000. The tax was later completely repealed in 1872. Abe was also the first Republican President of the United States, the more liberal party at the time.

1913 saw the return of the Personal income tax; becoming a permanent part of our nation's finance system. This time it was President Woodrow Wilson, a Democrat, thought of as the progressive party at the time.

The GOP has pushed through the first major tax reform in over 30 years. As CPAs, this is one of the most exciting times in our careers. Although we love the tax planning and strategies we work on with our clients, they don't change a lot from year to year. Any time there's a tax law change we get really excited to see how it's going to affect our clients. We have late night parties with our accountant friends (kidding) to talk about how each provision of the new law will change the tax situation for our clients and ourselves. Maybe this sounds like we are accounting nerds, and we are, but we really love this stuff!

In the chapters that follow, we will lay out most of the major changes that affect individuals and small businesses. It doesn't end there however. . . The changes for many of our clients may be substantial and may fundamentally change our tax strategies.

Streamlined? Simple? File your taxes on a notecard? We aren't there yet. Our practice isn't quite ready to close its doors. In fact, we suspect we will be busier than ever before as new planning opportunities take shape, and the implementation of the new tax bill raises more questions. When such a large portion of your earnings are withheld to support our government, we need to REALLY think and plan each financial transaction. We all want to support the system, but we certainly don't want to pay more than necessary.

CHAPTER TWO

TAX RATES

Boring... YES, the tax rates have changed and the new rates DEFINITELY have profound effects on all of us. That doesn't make it less boring. What REALLY matters is what income is taxed, at these new rates, and what deductions you get to take to arrive at your taxable income. Nevertheless, no tax update book would be complete without spending at least a little time on the new tax rates.

SEVEN different tax rates! We thought this was supposed to get easier? The truth is that computerized tax programs do all the calculations, so we don't really care how many there are. However, we DO care about what the end result will be. Let's take a look at the before and after table of tax rates:

TAX BRACKET FOR SINGLE FILERS

Current law		Final Plan	
10 %	$ 9,325 and below	10 %	$ 9,525 and below
15 %	$ 9,326 - $ 37,950	12 %	$ 9,526 - $ 38,700
25 %	$ 37,951 - $ 91,900	22 %	$ 38,701 - $ 82,500
28 %	$ 91,901 - $ 191,650	24 %	$ 82,501 - $ 157,500
33 %	$ 191,651 - $ 416,700	32 %	$ 157,501 - $ 200,000
35 %	$ 416,701 - $ 418,400	35 %	$ 200,001 - $ 500,00
39.6 %	$ 418,401 and up	37 %	$ 500,001 and up

Let's look at one happy taxpayer and see how the new tax law will change her taxes. Samantha works on campus at the bookstore after school. Her taxable income was $30,000. (NOTE: Samantha has dated the same guy for years, but she is still single and available.)

Under the current law she would pay 10% on the first $9,325 of income and 15% on the rest. Her taxes would be $933 on the first part and $3,101 on the second part, for a total tax of $4,034.

It looks like the new law will tax Samantha would pay 10% on the first $9525 of income and 12% on the rest. Her taxes would be $953 on the first part and $2,457 on the second part, for a total tax of $3,410. RIGHT?...WRONG.

STOP….. it's not that simple… You cannot just look at the tax bracket table to figure out if you will be paying more or less taxes. It is, of course, more complicated. Even in this VERY SIMPLE case where we have a single taxpayer with no other income, no home, no investments, and no side business, there's more to it. Let's explain. . .

When looking at the tax brackets and applying it to your income you must FIRST calculate your TAXABLE income? Your TAXABLE income is NOT how much you made.

In Samantha's case, her TAXABLE income, under the current law was $30,000. She actually made more than that, but after taking the personal exemption ($4,050) and standard deduction ($6,350) her 2017 taxable income was $30,000.

To give apples to apples, we have to start with her total earnings of $40,400 and take away the new standard deduction and personal exemption. Uh oh, part of the new law is that there are NO MORE PERSONAL EXEMPTIONS! Bad. But, the standard deduction is almost double for a single taxpayer. Good.

Here's how it REALLY works out for Samantha under the new tax law:

Gross Income:	$40,400
Less Standard deduction:	($12,000)
Equals TAXABLE income:	$28,400

Applying the new tax rates, Samantha would again pay $953 on the first $9,525 of income and 12% on the remaining $18,875. $953 + $2,265 = $3,218.

Samantha still WINS under the new tax law. She's also excited because the bookstore where she works is going to be paying a lower corporate tax rate and has promised to give everyone a $1 per hour raise. Samantha is now a converted republican (although she is still a student, so that could change with the wind.) She's signed up for an economics class taught by a famously liberal professor, Dr. Boesen, so she's expecting to hear all the bad news about the new tax bill and the economy. Professor Boesen could be right, the economy is very complicated and the implications of this tax law will have many effects that we don't yet understand. Samantha, for now, is happy. In her world things have gotten better, except she still has that boyfriend.

Long term capital gains and dividends

The simple headline is that capital gain rates have not changed. The new law preserves the existing 0%, 15% and 20% tax rates on long term capital gains and dividends. However, the brackets at which theses rates kick in have changed quite a bit. The new rate brackets are as follows:

Capital Gains Rate	Single	Joint	Head of Household
0% Bracket	$0 - $38,600	$0 - $77,200	$0 - $51,700
Beginning of 15% Bracket	$38,601	$77,201	$51,701
Beginning of 20% Bracket	$425,801	$479,001	$452,401

One proposed provision, which did NOT make it to the final bill, was the requirement to treat all stock sales on a first-in-first-out method. Inclusion of this provision would have resulted in maximizing your gain, and maximizing your corresponding tax liability.

CHAPTER THREE

HOMEOWNER TAX DEDUCTIONS

The House and Senate tax bills differed on what and how much could be deducted by homeowners. The deductibility of home mortgage interest is a sacred cow and they wouldn't dare take it away. Or would they. . .

Most taxpayers never realized that a limit on the deductibility of mortgage interest has been in place for years. Yes, it's true. If your mortgage is over one million dollars, the interest isn't deductible on any of the debt over one million. Even in Southern California there are not too many folks with mortgages over a million. Nevertheless, we do deal with quite a few clients who exceed this limitation, and cannot deduct some of their interest.

The new tax law was finalized, lowering the mortgage limit to $750,000. Again, that means that you cannot write off any interest on the portion of your loan that exceeds $750,000.

This limit would have only applied to a very small portion of loans originated between 2013 and 2015. According to the National Low Income Housing Coalition, only 1.9% of all loans in that time period exceeded the $750,000 maximum. California accounted for 45.7% of those loans, so this hits our state hard. Maybe we will convert from blue to red. Could this be a payback at California for our lack of support of the current administration?

Good news though. . . This does NOT apply to existing mortgages! If you had a large mortgage, 2017 would have been the time to refinance it. . .

So many decisions have been made based on being able to deduct the interest on our homes.

Making decisions based on tax consequences is called tax planning. It's important to understand how taxes affect your investments. We hate clichés, but this one does ring true: *Failing to plan, is planning to fail.*

How income and expenses are treated for tax purposes, can have a significant impact on your financial health. One client chose to obtain a home mortgage, rather than use accumulated cash to purchase a new home. She had accumulated substantial credit card debt and realized that the interest on credit cards in not deductible. Rather than use her cash to buy the home, she used it to pay off her credit cards. Not only was the interest on the home loan a tax deduction, but it was also at a much lower rate.

These tax decisions will become more difficult for many of us with the new tax law. Even if your mortgage interest IS on a loan of $750,000 or less, you may choose to take the standard deduction, if your itemized deductions are less than the threshold. That simple change in the standard deduction is a huge benefit to many but still has the ultimate effect of making the home mortgage interest deduction worthless for others.

So... IS THERE REALLY A TAX BENEFIT to owning a home? The answer of course is: "it depends." Let's look at some examples . . .

Taxpayers Amy and Andy own a home and have the following deductible expenses for their tax return:

Mortgage interest:	$9,709
Property taxes:	$4,800

Their total home related deductions are $14,509. Without anything else to deduct on their schedule A, they would be better off taking the standard deduction of $24,000. Note that the standard deduction for a single person is $12,000.

But wait, there's more . . . There are some other expenses that are deductible on Amy and Andy's Schedule A. If the TOTAL of all the itemized Schedule A deductions exceeds $24,000 then they will, of course, use the total Schedule A number. Most of these are covered in our chapter about Itemized Deductions.

In the case of Amy and Andy, they had also made a charitable deduction of $600 to their local Pet Rescue, and a Political Donation to the Trump Campaign of $3,000. Political contributions have never been deductible. However, including the charitable contribution, will bring their total itemized deductions to $15,109.

Amy and Andy opted to take the $24,000 standard deduction. However, they received NO BENEFIT from their property taxes, mortgage interest, or charitable contributions because even if all those numbers were zero, their taxes would not have changed.

Home Equity Interest

Who hasn't taken out a home equity loan to fix things up around the house? Home equity interest has always been a tax deduction, but no more. This is one of the items eliminated under the new tax law. If you have a $200,000 first mortgage and a $200,000 home equity loan then you might consider consolidating them into one single first mortgage, so you might still benefit from the entire interest deduction.

CHAPTER FOUR

STANDARD DEDUCTIONS AND ITEMIZED DEDUCTIONS

As you may already know, taxpayers are entitled to take either the standard deduction or the sum of their itemized deductions. The standard deduction is a dollar amount which reduces your taxable income, and is specified by the IRS. It lessens the need for taxpayers, with fewer deductions. to itemize actual expenses. Previously, the standard deduction was $ 6,350 for single taxpayers and $ 12,000 for married couples filing jointly. Under the new tax bill, taxpayers can now deduct almost double.. that's $12,000 for single filer, and $24,000 for a married couple.

Standard Deduction

Filing Status	Previous	New
Single or Married Filing Separately	$ 6,350	$ 12,000
Head of Household	$ 9,350	$ 18,000
Married Filing Jointly or Qualified Widower with dependent	$ 12,700	$ 24,000

*This table does not apply to taxpayers born before 1952, who are blind, or a dependent of another.

If your deductible expenses exceed the standard deduction, listed above, then itemizing deductions is the best fit for you. Taxpayers might previously deduct some medical and dental expenses, some taxes, interest, charitable contributions, casualty and theft losses, and many other miscellaneous items. There were already many limitations on how these deductions were calculated. The new tax bill has eliminated all of the miscellaneous deductions, increased the deductions for medical expenses, increased the limits of deductible contributions, and limited the deductibility of state and local taxes.

Deductible medical expenses have reverted back to the prior threshold of 7.5%, of Adjusted Gross Income, down from the current 10%. This means you will reach a level of deductibility sooner. This provision is retroactive to the 2017 tax year.

Under the final tax bill, state and local taxes are deductible up to $10,000. This includes property taxes on your personal residence, and your state income taxes paid. A painful hit to many Californians.

Charitable donations are now allowed up to 60% of your Adjusted Gross Income, an increase from 50%. Donations in excess of the limitation will continue to carry forward to future years. As more taxpayers will be using the increased standard deduction, rather than itemizing, this could translate into less contributions to charity. We hate to think that philanthropy is driven by taxes, but we are not that optimistic. In the long run, this could be bad news for some charitable organizations.

The prior limit on the total amount of allowable itemized deductions, and the related phase out of them, has been eliminated under the new tax bill.

See the HOMEOWNER TAX DEDUCTIONS chapter for a thorough discussion on property tax and mortgage interest

.

CHAPTER FIVE

PERSONAL EXEMPTION and CHILD TAX CREDITS

Personal Exemption

Gone. GONE. gone...

Of all the changes in tax reform, families will miss personal exemption the most. Taxpayers may benefit in doubling the standard deductions, but any change comes at a cost. Beginning 2018, the personal exemption of $4,050 for each taxpayer, spouse, and dependent has been eliminated.

This DOES make doing your taxes simpler... Anything they can get rid of helps simplify the tax code and the process of preparing tax returns. Although this, by itself, is a painful benefit to remove, the increased standard deduction is intended to be the offset.

Let's look at an example to better understand this exemption.

Let's say Archie and Amber are married filing jointly with 4 kids and adjusted gross income of $60,000. Previously, they could deduct $24,300 in personal exemptions ($4,050 per person) and $12,700 in standard deduction, for a total of $37,000. After passing the new tax law, they can only deduct a total standard deduction of $24,000, and $0 personal exemption.

Child Tax Credits

There is great news with the Child Tax Credit. It is now doubled for children under 17 years old. You now get a $2,000 credit per qualifying child. For other dependents, taxpayers will get a $500 credit. However, the portion of the child credit which was previously refundable (as it can be refunded even if you have not tax liability) is now part of the $2,000, rather than an additional amount.

Let's translate Archie and Amber's situation into tax dollars. Under the prior law the personal exemptions would have resulted in a taxable income of $23,000. The tax on this amount would be $2,521, which would be completely offset by the available child tax credit. The additional refundable child tax credit would have yielded a refund of $1,480.

Under the newly passed tax law, the allowable standard deduction would have resulted in taxable income of $36,000. The tax on this amount would be $4,130. The child tax credit would completely eliminate this tax liability and actually leave them with a tax credit that is refundable to them. Recall that earlier we explained a REFUNDABLE credit was one that could give you more money back than you even paid in taxes originally. Here, the Child Tax Credit is a refundable credit but only at $1400 per child. (meaning that only $1400 of the $2000 is refundable)

The tax law changes for Archie and Amber would be VERY beneficial because they would end up with a refund of $3870 and be voting Republican for the first time ever.

CHAPTER SIX

CASUALTY LOSSES

Possibly one of the last deductions you will ever want to use is the one for casualty, disaster, and theft losses. These events typically result in damage, destruction, or loss of property resulting from an identifiable event that is sudden, unexpected, or unusual.

For example, items that typically meet the criteria for losses are included below:

Casualty and disaster losses

-Car accidents
-Disaster-related demolition
-Earthquakes
-Fires
-Floods
-Hurricanes
-Shipwrecks
-Storms
-Terrorist attacks
-Tornadoes
-Vandalism
-Volcanic eruptions

Theft losses

-Blackmail
-Burglary
-Embezzlement
-Extortion
-Kidnapping
-Larceny
-Robbery

Casualty, disaster, and theft losses are categorized as either business or personal casualty losses. We will summarize the changes for business clients in another upcoming booklet. For personal casualty losses, you previously MUST have itemized your deductions to take any deduction for the loss. The deduction was limited to amounts over $100 that exceeded 10% of your adjusted gross income.

The deductions for most casualty and theft losses are NO LONGER allowed if the losses occur after December 31, 2017. A deduction is now allowable only for losses attributable to a presidentially declared disaster.

Casualty, disaster, and theft losses will still have an impact on you even if it is not a situation that is declared a major disaster by the President. For the best possible protection it is a good idea to insure that high value assets like your home, recreational vehicles, etc. are properly covered by insurance policies. There's always going to be some event that you didn't insure against. For instance, most insurance policies do not provide insurance for terrorist attacks, acts of God, kidnapping, or extortion. Despite your efforts, you can't cover everything and the Government will no longer be your partner in your loss. It's YOUR loss and they aren't going to give you any tax benefit for the loss. You're on your own now.

CHAPTER SEVEN

EDUCATION CREDITS, TUITION REIMBURSEMENTS AND STUDENT LOAN INTEREST

Very little is changing here. There was talk of consolidating the American Opportunity Tax Credit and the Lifetime Learning Credit and adding a fifth year with half the benefits, as well as repealing the tax deduction for interest paid on federal student loans. None of these provisions made it to the final bill.

Another valuable tool, which has remained unchanged, relates to employer provided educational assistance. An employer can still provide educational assistance up to

$5,250, per year, tax free to the employee. If you are considering returning to school, or finishing that degree, it may be mutually beneficial to ask your employer for educational assistance, rather than a raise.

A change that WILL be implemented is a modification of the exclusion of student loan discharges from gross income. Certain discharges, on account of death or disability, will be excluded from income as part of the new tax bill.

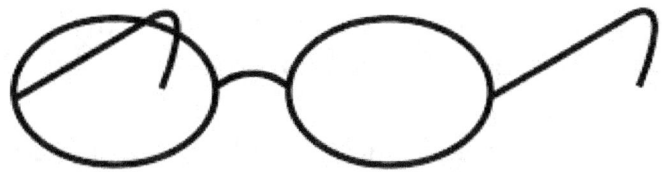

CHAPTER EIGHT

ALTERNATIVE MINIMUM TAX

Alternative Minimum Tax (AMT) was created in the 1960s to prevent high-income taxpayers from avoiding individual income tax. High-income taxpayers calculate their tax liability under the ordinary income tax system and again under the AMT. The taxpayer then pays the higher of the two. Basically, high-income taxpayers have an additional level of complexity in preparing their tax returns, While we were hopeful that "simplification" would eliminate AMT from the tax code, no such luck.

The new tax law somewhat softens the blow of the AMT. The new tax act did increase the income level at which a taxpayer is required to calculate the AMT, possibly reducing the number of individuals subject to the AMT.

The amount of income which would be exempt from AMT will be $55,400 for single taxpayers, and $86,200 for joint taxpayers. By most people's standards, these amounts are hardly what we consider "high-income." The AMT will begin to phase out at an income level of $120,700 for single filers, and $160,900 for joint filers. At these amounts the regular tax will equal or exceed the AMT.

The AMT provisions, in the tax bill, will expire in 2025, and revert to the pre-2018 law, unless Congress extends or replaces this provision.

CHAPTER NINE

VARIOUS OTHER ISSUES

529 College savings plans: The tax bill provides more flexibility in the use of 529 college savings plans. Currently, earnings from 529 plans and distributions for qualified education expenses are not taxable. The new law expands the definition of "qualified educational expenses" to include payments to elementary and secondary schools. The non-taxable distribution would be limited to $10,000, per student, per year. This limitation does not apply to post-secondary school expenses.

Alimony: Previous law allowed the deductibility of alimony payments, and these amounts were also includable in the recipient's income. The new tax bill repeals this, eliminating both the deduction, and inclusion, for divorce or separation agreements executed after December 31st, 2018. Agreements already in effect will adhere to the old rules, unless modified after December 31, 2018. Sometimes a big part of tax planning includes marriage (and divorce) planning. If you are contemplating the latter, perhaps you should evaluate the timing with your CPA and your attorney.

Child tax credit: The tax bill increases the child tax credit to $2,000 per qualifying child. The maximum refundable amount of this credit is $1,400, meaning you can collect it even if you do not have a tax liability. The bill will also introduce a new nonrefundable $500 credit for qualifying dependents who are not qualifying children.

Educator's expenses: The tax bill did not change the allowable $250 deduction for K-12 educators' expenses incurred for the purchase of classroom materials.

Exclusion for bicycle commuting reimbursements: The tax bill has revoked the exclusion from gross income of qualified bicycle commuting expenses through 2025.

Home equity loans: The tax bill has revoked the home-equity loan interest deduction through 2025. There is NO grandfather clause with this law so this DOES apply to existing home equity loans. Now is the time to consider getting these paid off, since the interest you pay will no longer be deductible.. We often help clients decide if they should keep these loans and use the money to invest in other things. That entire analysis now changes because the interest is no longer deductible. Maybe now is the time to get more conservative with your investments and use that spare cash to pay off your home equity loan instead of investing in your brother-in-law's snow cone business.

Medical expenses: The new tax bill reduces the threshold for the deductibility of medical expenses to 7.5% of adjusted gross income. This is the only provision of the bill which will be in effect for the 2017 tax year as well.

Miscellaneous Itemized deductions: The tax bill has revoked all miscellaneous itemized deductions subject to the 2% floor under the current law, through 2025. This is a BIG deal for some people. We often see salespeople, who are paid on a W2 but spend a lot of their personal money on meals, supplies, entertaining, and other items related to their job.

Moving expenses: The tax bill has revoked moving expense deductions through 2025. The tax bill has also revoked the exclusion from gross income for qualified moving expense reimbursements. Exceptions apply to members of the armed forces.

Sale of a principal residence: The tax bill did not change the current tax rules on exclusion of gain from the sale of a principal residence. Both the House and Senate proposals included some change in this area. Fortunately none of these made it to the final bill. Homeowners will still be allowed the exclusion of gain on sale, $250,000 for single filers and $500,000 for married. The occupancy requirements are also unchanged..

Other credits for Individuals: The tax bill preserves credits for plug-in electric drive motor vehicles and adoption expenses.

CHAPTER TEN

ESTATE TAX ISSUES

Previously, estates generally paid 40 percent federal tax on inherited property, but the law waives that tax for estates up to $5,600,000. This baseline exemption is doubling to $11,200,000.

With the use of proper planning, couples may be able to shield up to $22.4 million in total estate value. These new rules apply to the estate, gift, and generation-skipping taxes for people who die after December 31, 2017 but before January 1, 2026. This may indicate that death planning could be as important as tax, marriage or divorce planning.

CHAPTER ELEVEN

EXCISE TAXES THAT AFFECT US ALL

What are excise taxes? Who pays them?

Excise taxes are added to the cost of a product at the wholesale or distributor level and are included in the retail price you pay for good before the sales taxes are added.

Perhaps the MOST IMPORTANT change comes in the reduction of the excise tax on beer and wine. Our friends Arvon and Rosanne are going to enjoy this provision almost as much as their daughters Wendy and Kelly.

Included in the tax bill is *The Craft Beverage Modernization and Tax Reform Act.*

As part of the new tax law, we will enjoy the first reduction in wine excise taxes in over 80 years. This mainly helps the small producers because the credit applies to the first 750,000 gallons of wine.

The excise tax on beer is reduced from $7 per barrel to $3.50 per barrel on the first 60,000 barrels. This ONLY applies to brewers that brew LESS than 2 million barrels per year through 2019. This is TRULY a tax benefit for the little guy and helps them compete with the more efficient mega-brewers by giving them a $3.50 cut per barrel on production. Every penny counts in this business.

Similar savings are also available for certain distilled spirits.

Excise tax on Highly Compensated Nonprofit Employees

There's nothing worse than making a charitable deduction and later finding out that the CEO is making over a million dollars in wages. This leaves a bad taste in your mouth, and possibly inhibits future donations. There are so many great charities out there and we encourage you to do some research before giving away your hard earned money.

Another great WIN in this tax bill is the PENALTY Excise tax of 21% on compensation in excess of $1,000,000 paid by tax-exempt organizations to their covered employees.

You could argue correctly that this tax drains even MORE money from the charity and further prevents them from fulfilling their charitable purpose. We might argue that it could make the charitable organization boards review their salary policies, and perhaps put more of your donations to work as you intended. For those organizations that end up paying, rest assured that the IRS will make good choices on where to spend this tax.

Or will they?

CHAPTER TWELVE

BUSINESS TAXES

The most sweeping reform of the US tax code in more than 30 years brings big changes for business.

C-Corps

For Corporations, the graduated tax rates of the past have been replaced with a flat rate of 21%. Previously the top rate was 35%. This is a massive change that our lawmakers hope will have a huge impact to motivate corporations to keep their profits in the USA instead of moving profitable companies offshore to lower taxed countries. This is a hotly debated topic. Will it really work? Our firm has high hopes for this but it will be hard to measure its success.

Many of our clients might consider changing their business to a C-CORP to take advantage of the reduced tax rates. There are lots of benefits, timing opportunities, and some pitfalls to this strategy and we're really looking forward to the tax planning challenge in 2018.

Flow throughs and Sole Proprietors

Unlike Corporations, flow through entities will continue to be taxed at the individual taxpayer level and so they will NOT enjoy the benefit of the lowered tax rate for Corporations. Flow through entities include Partnerships, LLCs and S-Corporations.

These flow through entities AND sole proprietorships will enjoy another huge new benefit. They can all exclude 20% of their business income from being taxed. Let's look at this in a bit more detail:

Maritza owns a small flower shop and reports the income on Schedule C of her individual tax return. After all expenses, her net income for 2017 was $50,000. She'll pay tax on that full amount. In 2018, assuming her net income is exactly the same, she will get a 20% exclusion meaning she is only taxed on 80% of the $50,000 which is $40,000.

NOT SO FAST…. it sounds great but this 20% exclusion doesn't apply to ALL businesses. Here's who it DOESN'T apply to:

> Any trade or business involving the performance of services in the fields of health, law, accounting, actuarial science, performing arts, consulting, athletics, financial services, brokerage services, or any trade or business where the principal asset of such trade or business is the reputation or skill of 1 or more of its employees.

Yikes! So just about any service business will NOT get the benefit of this. As accountants, we do not get the benefit.

Again… another exception: The 20% exclusion IS going to be allowed for the disallowed fields of business if their total taxable income falls below $315,000 for married taxpayers and $157,500 for all others. That's right. . . . ANOTHER win for the little guy. **This is significant.**

You could have some tax planning to do here. If your taxable income is ABOVE the threshold, you need to map out how much to pay yourself on W2 vs taking dividends from the company in order to maximize the 20% exclusion.

There are a lot of calculations and limitations to this new 20% exclusion. Don't be surprised if what looks good at first glance ends up not helping you. As accounting professionals, we certainly would have preferred some other outcome.

ABOUT THE AUTHORS

Having met in college, Patrick and Julie both pursued careers in public accounting, each working for one of the top eight accounting firms worldwide. After working in various arenas, from public accounting to public education, and healthcare to real estate, Patrick and Julie finally joined forces professionally when they opened Gentile, McCloskey and Company in 2004. Patrick and Julie are both active members of the community, sitting on various charitable boards and participating in many local events. With over 40 years of combined experience in the accounting, tax, and business management fields, Patrick and Julie service a broad range of clients from their office in Old Town Monrovia. They provide advice and strategic tax planning for their tax clients as part of preparing corporate, partnership, individual, and fiduciary tax returns.

With credentials as long as your arm, including contractor's licenses, a real estate broker's license, two masters degrees, a juris doctorate, and postgraduate doctoral studies, Patrick and Julie could bore you with bios for days. They would much rather meet you in person so you can see they are just regular working class stiffs who really enjoy helping their clients navigate the everyday tax issues that affect most of us.

We hope you enjoyed this little book, as much as one can enjoy this many words about taxes. If you would like more information about Gentile, McCloskey and Company or Patrick and Julie, please visit our website at www.gmtaxes.com.

"The taxpayer: that's someone who works for the federal government, but doesn't have to take the civil service examination." — Ronald Reagan

"The hardest thing in the world to understand is the income tax." — Albert Einstein

www.ingramcontent.com/pod-product-compliance
Lightning Source LLC
Chambersburg PA
CBHW071234220526
45468CB00002B/852